weird but true! 7

THAT'S WEIRD!

NATIONAL GEOGRAPHIC KiDS

weird but true! 7

300 outrageous facts

NATIONAL GEOGRAPHIC
WASHINGTON, D.C.

NEW
YORK

On average, the **Empire State Building** in New York City is hit by **lightning** 25 times a year.

AN ITALIAN DESIGNER MADE A COUCH SHAPED LIKE A CHOCOLATE BAR.

RED-FOOTED TORTOISES HAVE BEEN TAUGHT TO USE TOUCH SCREENS.

Sitting in a cardboard box can lower stress for domestic cats.

Your brain makes up only 2 percent of your total body weight but uses up to 20 percent of your body's energy.

HONEYBEES HAVE TWO STOMACHS.

Some frogs have green bones.

GOLDEN ORB-WEAVING SPIDERS
THAT LIVE IN
CITIES
GROW BIGGER
THAN ONES IN
RURAL AREAS.

SARCASTIC FRINGEHEAD FISH BATTLE OVER TURF BY WRESTLING EACH OTHER WITH THEIR MOUTHS.

THE HEAVIEST **CAULIFLOWER** ON RECORD WEIGHED MORE **THAN A BULLDOG.**

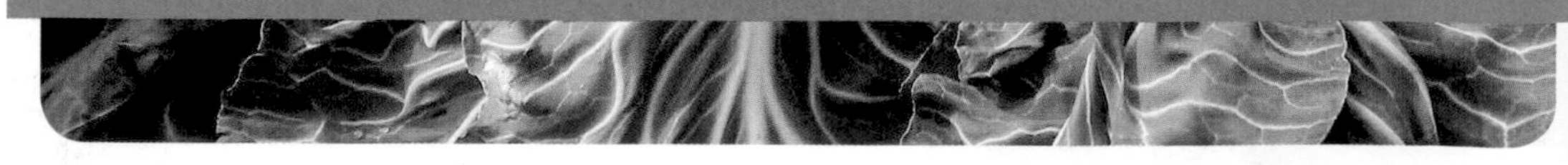

UP TO HALF OF THE WATER ON EARTH IS OLDER THAN THE SUN, ACCORDING TO ONE STUDY.

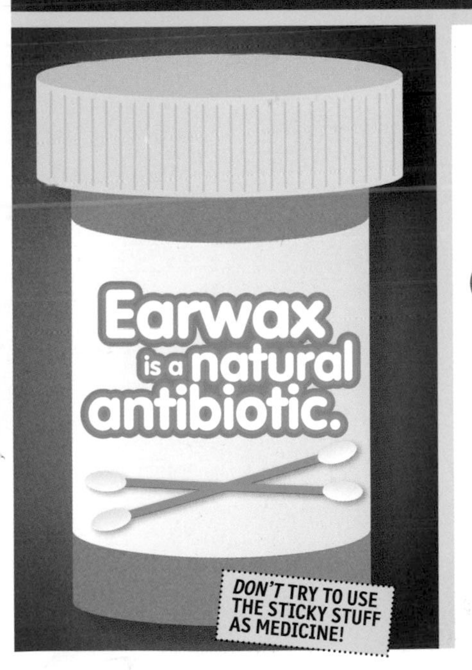

Food travels through your esophagus at a speed of about one inch (2.5 cm) a second.

3,000,000,000

MORE THAN
THREE BILLION
PASSENGERS TRAVEL ON
COMMERCIAL AIRPLANES
EVERY YEAR.

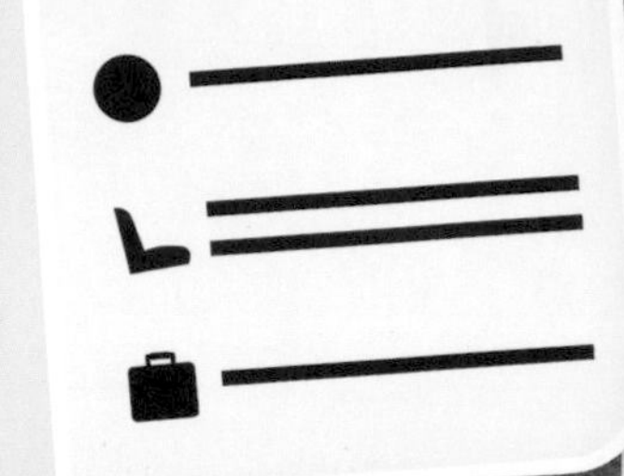

A STUDY FOUND THAT **CHEWING GUM** PUTS YOU IN A **BETTER MOOD.**

ONE MAN INVENTED **A SUPERFAST POTATO PEELER** OUT OF A TOILET BRUSH ATTACHED TO A DRILL.

A SPANISH SCIENTIST INVENTED ICE CREAM THAT CHANGES COLORS WHEN LICKED.

THE PUDU—
A SMALL
KIND OF DEER—
RUNS IN A
ZIGZAG
PATTERN
TO ESCAPE
PREDATORS.

YOU HAVE TASTE RECEPTORS IN YOUR STOMACH.

SPITTING SPIDERS IMMOBILIZE PREY BY SPRAYING THEM WITH POISONOUS FLUID.

It takes more than ten gallons (38 L) of water to make one slice of bread.

The average wait time
at a fast-food
burger restaurant
drive-through is
203 seconds.

SPECIAL
VENDING MACHINES
IN ISTANBUL, TURKEY,
AUTOMATICALLY DISPENSE
FOOD AND WATER
FOR DOGS.

KARTAL BELEDİYESİ
KARTAL BELEDİYESİ
Çöpe atmayalım, Ayıralım,
Geleceğimizi Geri Kazanalım
Alo Çevre : 280 60 60
www. kartal.bel.tr
www.twitter.com/kartalbld
www.facebook.com/kartalbld
Karnım tok
keyfim yerinde

KARTAL BELEDİYESİ
Çöpe Atma
Buraya at

Cockroaches that lived 250 million years ago were as big as today's house cats.

ME-EW!

ARTIST CHARLES M. SCHULZ CREATED NEARLY 18,000 "PEANUTS" COMIC STRIPS.

Some airplane pilots use a beach on Fraser Island, Australia, as a landing strip.

Scientists have found a way to return hard-boiled egg whites to liquid form.

PASSENGERS ARRIVING AT ONE **NEW ZEALAND AIRPORT** ARE GREETED BY A **14-FOOT** (4.3-m) **BUST** OF THE **DRAGON**

Smaug **FROM *THE HOBBIT*** MOVIE TRILOGY.

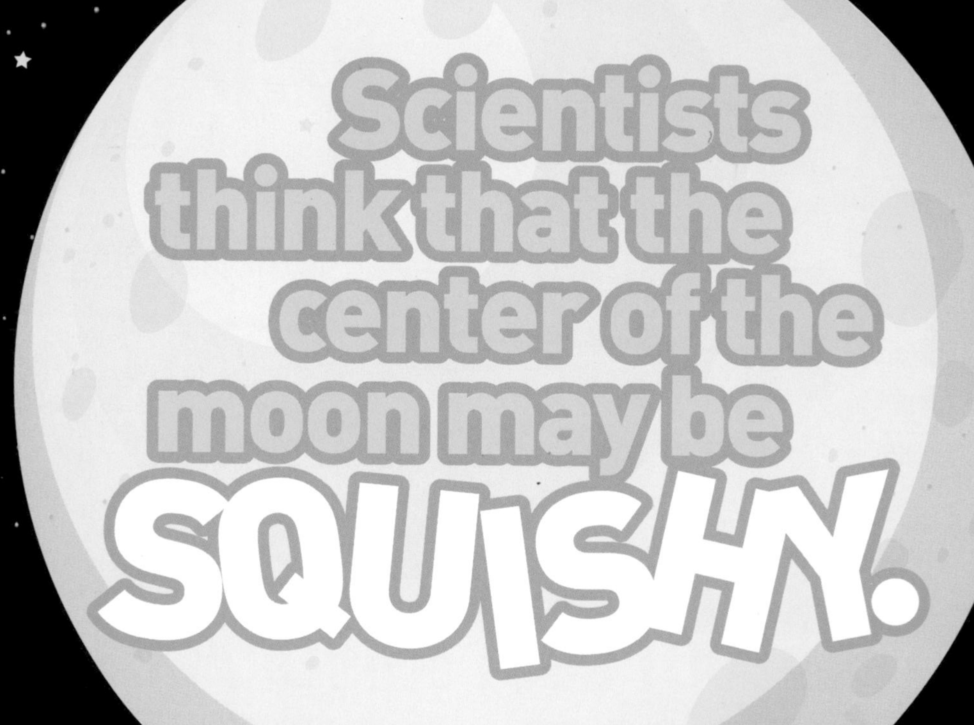
Scientists think that the center of the moon may be
SQUISHY.

IF THE DORMANT **SUPER-VOLCANO** IN YELLOWSTONE NATIONAL PARK, U.S.A., EVER **ERUPTED,** IT WOULD LIKELY SPEW ENOUGH **ASH** TO COVER ALL OF **NORTH AMERICA.**

The Pac-Man frog can lift three times its own **body weight** with its tongue.

LISTENING TO CLASSICAL MUSIC CAN HELP DOGS RELAX, A STUDY FOUND.

A DUTCH COMPANY PLANS TO BUILD A **SNOWFLAKE-SHAPED HOTEL** THAT FLOATS ON **WATER.**

THIS IS THE DESIGN FOR
THE HOTEL. COOL, HUH?

A NEWSPAPER IN SRI LANKA

was printed with insect-repelling ink to keep readers from getting bug bites.

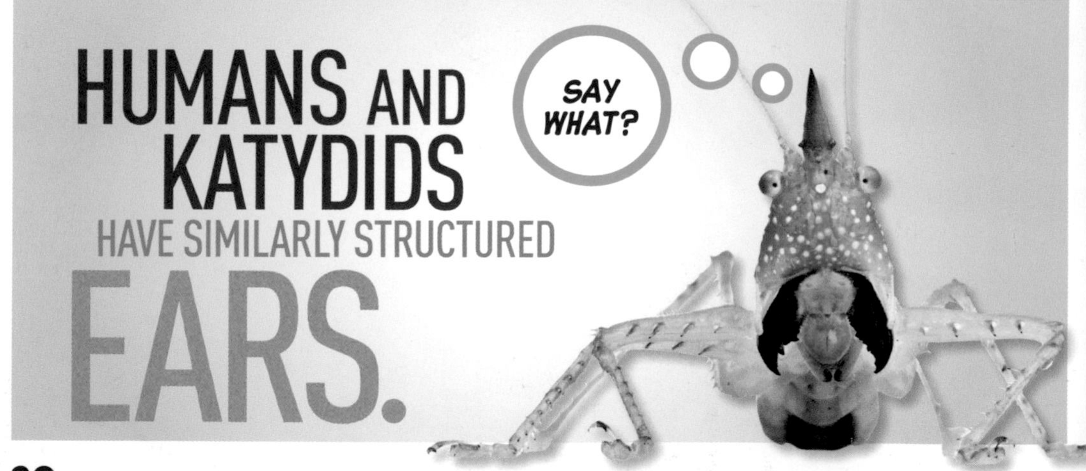

HUMANS AND KATYDIDS HAVE SIMILARLY STRUCTURED EARS.

THE GIANT PITCHER PLANT SECRETES NECTAR TO LURE BUGS AND RODENTS INTO ITS "MOUTH."

A record 232 people did a cannonball dive all at once into a harbor in New Zealand.

Between 1886 and 1902, the Statue of Liberty was used as a lighthouse.

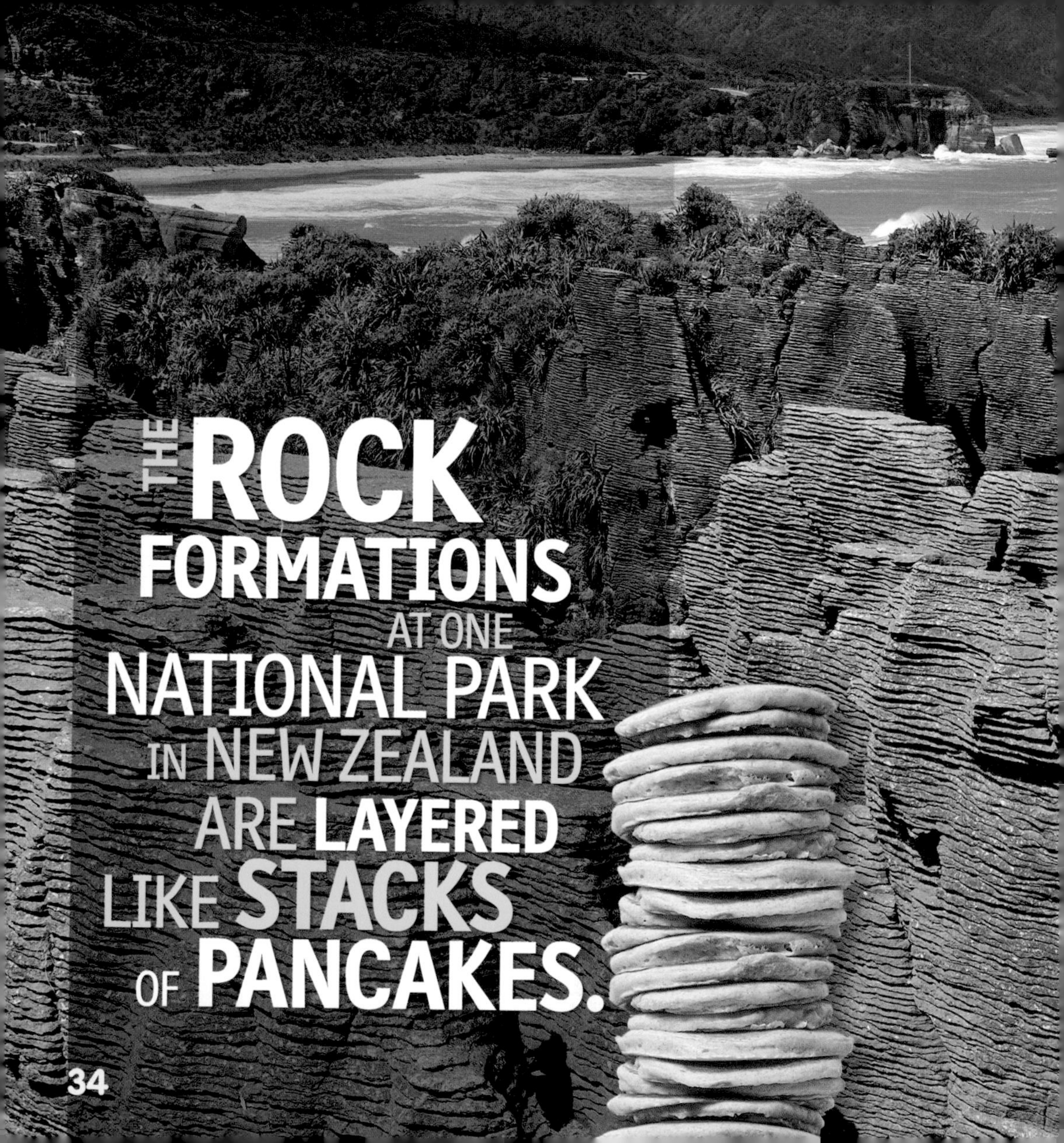

THE ROCK FORMATIONS AT ONE NATIONAL PARK IN NEW ZEALAND ARE LAYERED LIKE STACKS OF PANCAKES.

GIANT CUTTLEFISH HAVE BAGEL-SHAPED BRAINS.

During the
Ice Age,
supersize
lions
roamed
what is
now the
United Kingdom.

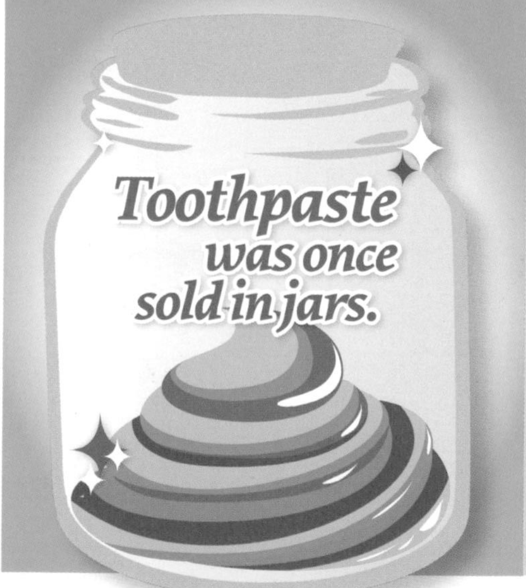
Toothpaste
was once
sold in jars.

HUMMINGBIRDS
FLAP THEIR
WINGS UP
TO
80 TIMES
A SECOND.

IT WOULD TAKE A SPACESHIP ABOUT 450 MILLION YEARS TO REACH THE EDGE OF OUR GALAXY.

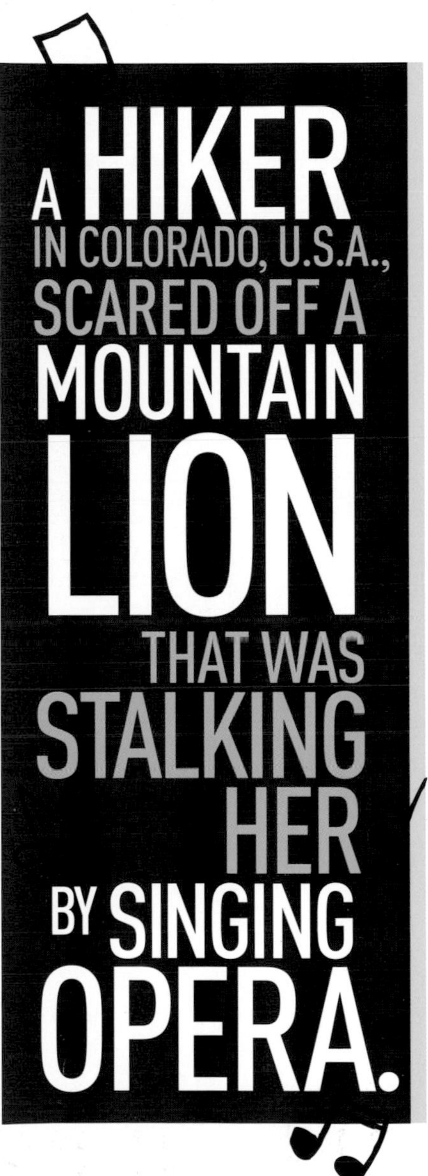

A KIND OF BIRD THAT LIVED 25 MILLION YEARS AGO HAD A WINGSPAN LONGER THAN SIX BASEBALL BATS.

SOME RAINBOWS APPEAR TO

CONTAIN ONLY SHADES OF RED.

About
6,000 hours
of new videos
are posted to
YouTube
every hour.

ONE WOMAN WALKED 10,000 MILES (16,093 km) ACROSS ASIA AND AUSTRALIA IN THREE YEARS.

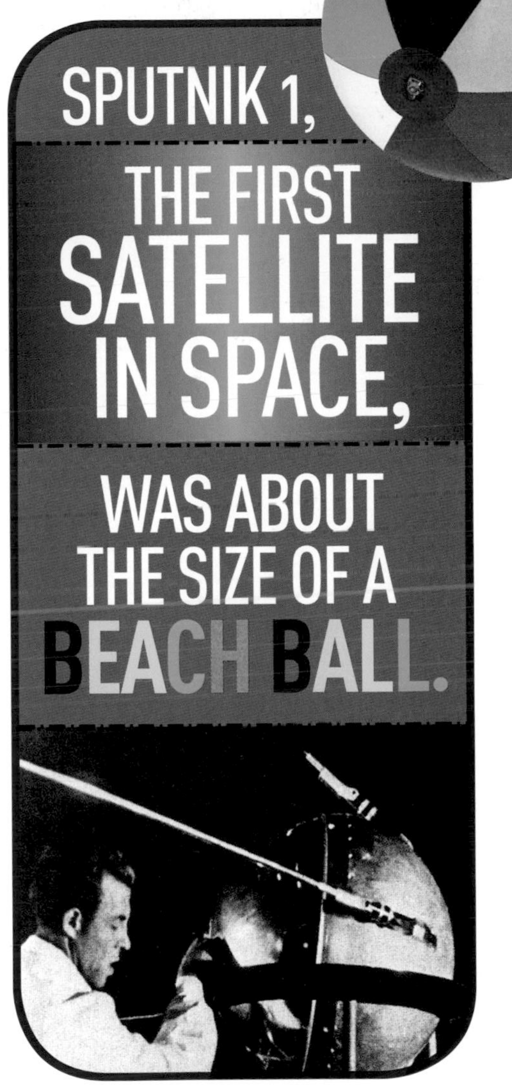

At an annual race in Totnes, England, competitors kick oranges along the course as they run.

On average, a $1 bill is in circulation in the United States for about six years.

The first

item sold on eBay was a broken laser pointer.

A cobra bit a chef in China 20 minutes AFTER its head had been CUT from its body.

EACH YEAR, WINDS BLOW ABOUT 40 MILLION TONS OF DUST (36 million t) FROM AFRICA'S SAHARA ...

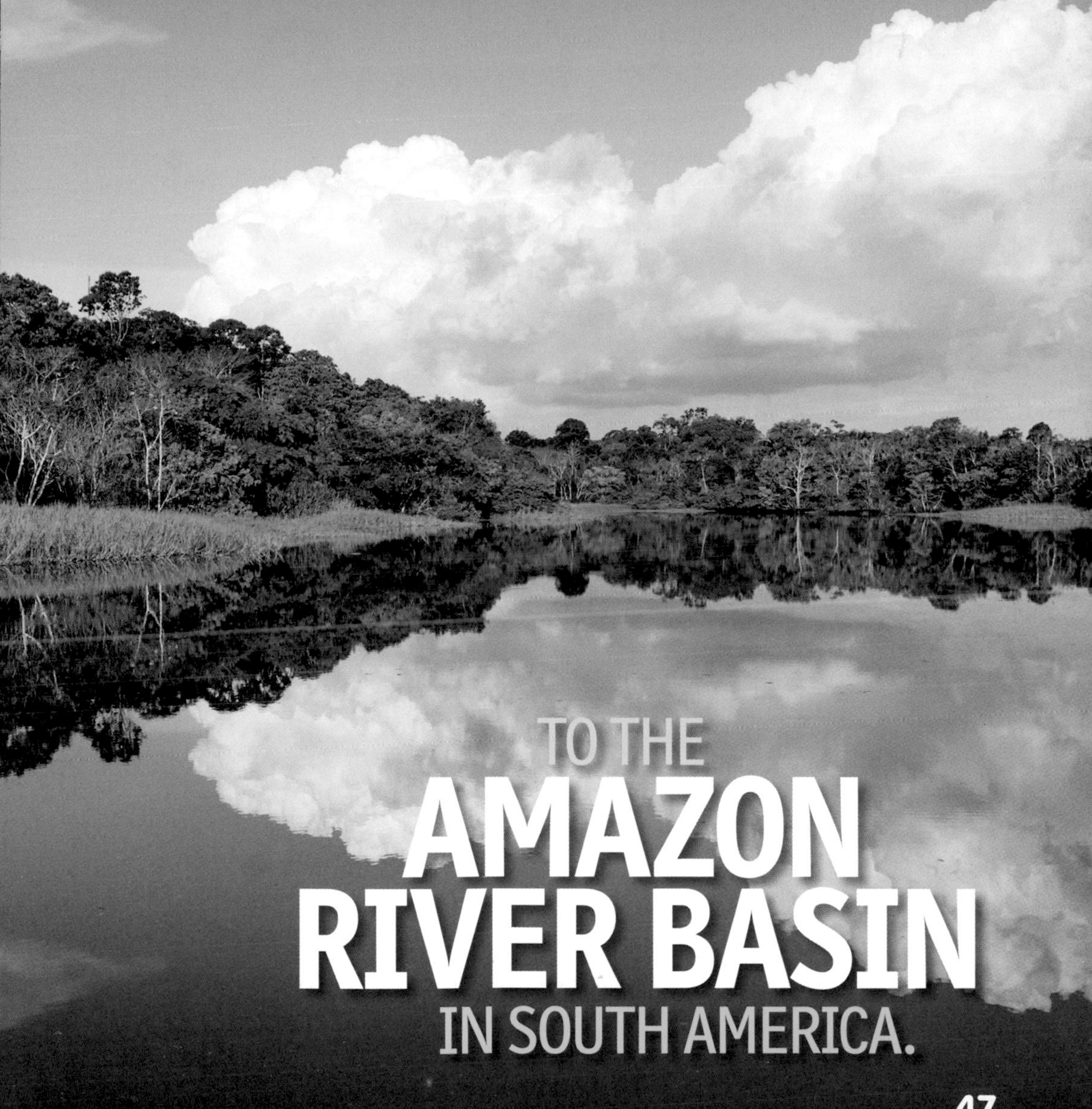

TO THE
AMAZON RIVER BASIN
IN SOUTH AMERICA.

There are
more than
20,000
TV stations
in the world.

FOUND IN AUSTRALIA AND NEW GUINEA, THE SOUTHERN CASSOWARY BIRD HAS CLAWS NEARLY THE LENGTH OF AN iPHONE.

The coati,
a member of
the raccoon family,
can rotate its ankles
180 degrees.

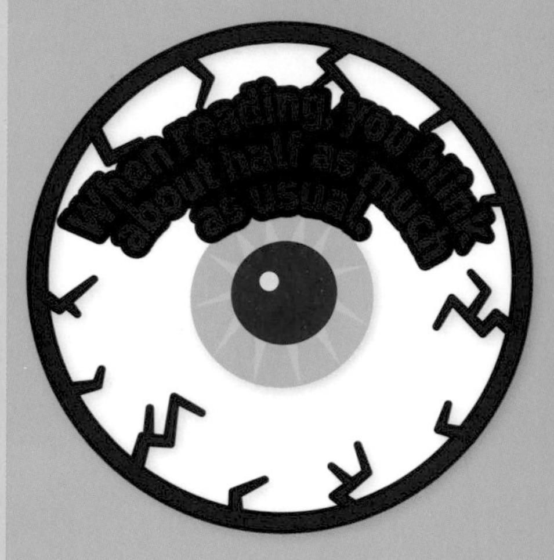
When reading, you blink about half as much as usual.

MORE THAN
29,000
GRAINS ARE IN A
ONE-POUND (0.5-kg)
BAG OF RICE.

A
HEXAGON-SHAPED HURRICANE
HAS HOVERED OVER SATURN'S NORTH POLE FOR AT LEAST
30 YEARS.

SCIENTISTS THINK OUR SUN HAS A "SIBLING"— A STAR 110 LIGHT-YEARS AWAY

THAT WAS BORN FROM THE SAME ANCIENT GAS CLOUD.

ILLUSTRATION OF THE SUN'S SIBLING STAR AND AN ORBITING PLANET

A group of Twitter users in Japan once posted 143,199 tweets in one second.

A STUDY FOUND THAT THE LONGER YOU SLEEP, THE STRANGER YOUR DREAMS BECOME.

VOLCANOES ONCE ERUPTED ON THE MOON.

Hello Kitty's full name is Kitty White.

MAY IMPROVE YOUR MEMORY.

Tortoises can crawl about one mile an hour.
(1.6 km/h)
WAIT FOR ME, GUYS!

A FRESHWATER LAKE THE SIZE OF LAKE ONTARIO IS HIDDEN UNDER NEARLY 2.5 MILES OF ICE (4 km) IN ANTARCTICA.

More American cash is spent outside the United States than inside its borders.

At the Starbucks in CIA headquarters, in Virginia, U.S.A., workers aren't allowed to write customers' names on cups.

THESE PLANT
CAN KILL

THE POISON GARDEN IN NORTH ENGLAND IS A PUBLIC GARDEN FILLED WITH DEADLY PLANTS.

On Christmas Island in the Indian Ocean, **red crabs outnumber** people by about **29,000 to 1.**

FLASHES OF LIGHT SOMETIMES APPEAR IN THE SKY BEFORE AND DURING EARTHQUAKES.

A WIND TURBINE IN DENMARK IS AS TALL AS A 72-STORY BUILDING.

THE ARCHES OF A McDONALD'S IN SEDONA, ARIZONA, U.S.A., ARE TURQUOISE INSTEAD OF YELLOW.

A CHOCOLATE BAR NAMED CHICKEN DINNER USED TO BE SOLD IN THE UNITED STATES.

Just a teaspoon (5 mL) of a neutron star's matter would weigh six billion tons. (5.5 billion t)

About 50 million inhabitants of the United States don't use the Internet—that's more people than the entire population of Argentina.

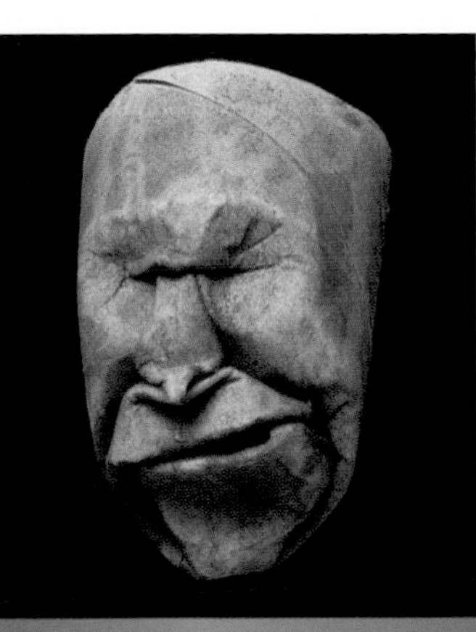

ONE FRENCH ARTIST CREATES **FACE MASKS** USING **TOILET PAPER ROLLS.**

A GROUP OF GOATS

IS CALLED A TRIP.

In **Japan,** you can **buy doughnuts stuffed** with **ramen noodles.**

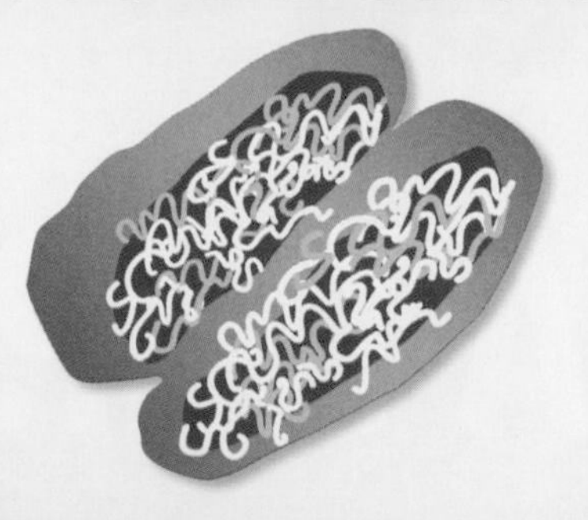

A **POMERANIAN** BECAME THE **FASTEST DOG** ON TWO PAWS AFTER WALKING NEARLY **33 FEET** (10 M) IN LESS THAN SEVEN SECONDS ON HIS **HIND LEGS.**

THE U.S. SUPREME COURT BUILDING IN WASHINGTON, D.C., HAS A BASKETBALL COURT ON ITS TOP FLOOR.

NEW YORK CITY'S **NEW YEAR'S EVE BALL** IS MADE UP OF

2,688

CRYSTAL PANELS.

A STUDY FOUND THAT
BABIES BORN IN WINTER
TEND TO CRAWL SOONER THAN
BABIES BORN IN SUMMER.

A Dutch artist created a 69-foot-long (21-m) wooden hippo and floated it down London's River Thames.

A **FARMER** IN CHINA GROWS **PEARS** SHAPED LIKE **BABIES.**

Restaurant diners who sit by a window tend to order salads more often, according to one study.

Osprey birds build nests big enough to fit an adult human inside.

Walt Disney World's Cinderella Castle contains a hotel suite that sleeps six people.

A company in the Middle East makes bodysuits for camels to wear while training for races.

THE **AMAZON RAIN FOREST** IS ABOUT TWICE THE SIZE OF INDIA.

MORE THAN **100 MILLION YEARS AGO,** INDIA WAS AN ISLAND.

Male walruses make a bell-like sound to attract mates.

Some **squat lobsters**—a kind of crustacean—are covered in **hairlike bristles.**

A MAN IN ILLINOIS, U.S.A., BUILT A PICKUP **TRUCK** THAT LOOKS AS IF IT HAS BEEN **FLIPPED** UPSIDE DOWN.

ZUCCHINIS ARE ABOUT
95 PERCENT WATER.

YOU'RE
30 TIMES
MORE LIKELY TO
LAUGH
WHEN YOU'RE
AROUND
FRIENDS
THAN WHEN
YOU'RE
ALONE.

Hagfish
digest
food
through
their
skin.

Mexico once had three different presidents in power in one day.

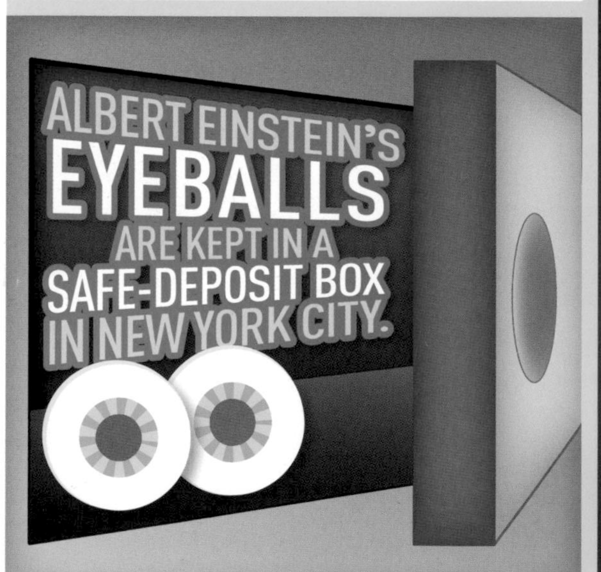

The world's loudest bicycle horn is louder than an ambulance siren.

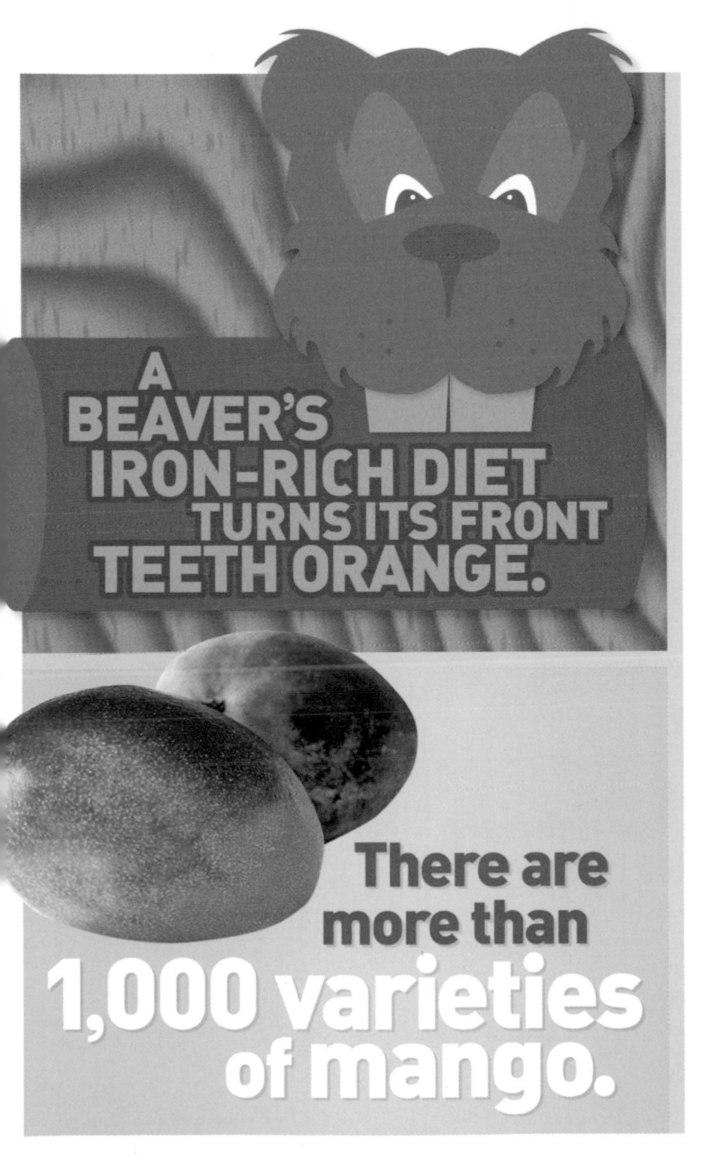
A BEAVER'S IRON-RICH DIET TURNS ITS FRONT TEETH ORANGE.
There are more than 1,000 varieties of mango.

IN 12TH-CENTURY CHINA,
PEOPLE WORE SUNGLASSES WITH LENSES MADE FROM QUARTZ,
A TYPE OF CRYSTAL.

Australia's Great Barrier Reef is roughly the size of Italy.

83

A **crosswalk light** in Lisbon, Portugal, features a figure **dancing to music** as the **stop signal.**

SOME **POLICE CARS** IN DUBAI, UNITED ARAB EMIRATES, CAN GO MORE THAN **220 MILES** (354 km/h) AN HOUR.

THERE ARE
FIVE TIMES
AS MANY
BICYCLES
AS CARS IN
COPENHAGEN,
DENMARK.

IT'S IMPOSSIBLE
FOR A BAT TO STAND
UPRIGHT.

TOGETHER, A
TARSIER'S
EYES
WEIGH NEARLY AS
MUCH AS
ITS BRAIN.
As a training tool, the U.S. military
created a plan to
combat zombies.

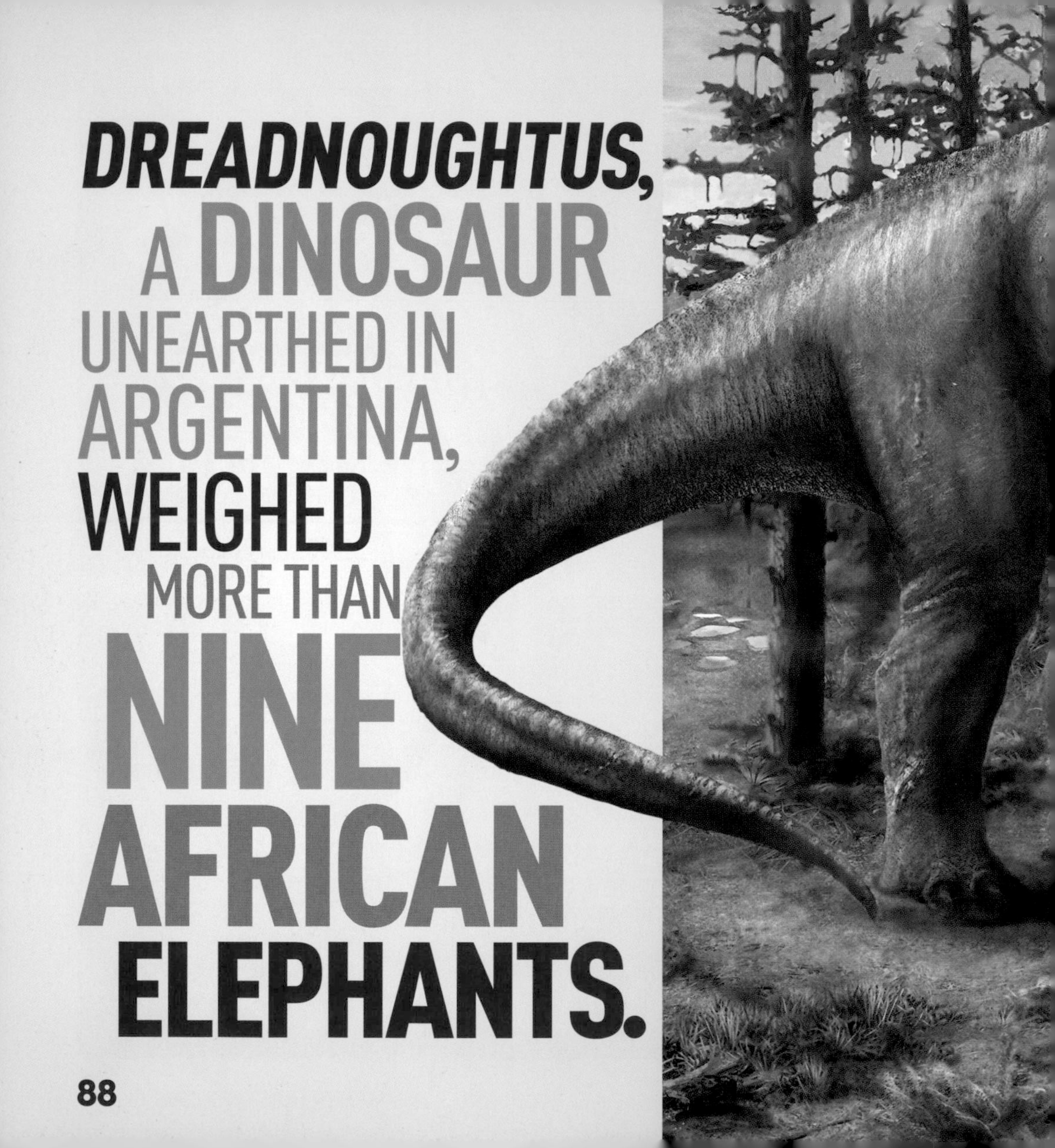

DREADNOUGHTUS, A **DINOSAUR** UNEARTHED IN ARGENTINA, **WEIGHED** MORE THAN **NINE AFRICAN ELEPHANTS.**

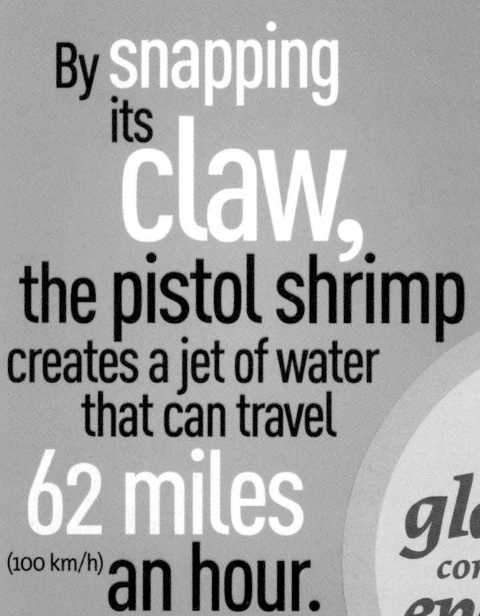

By **snapping** its **claw,** the pistol shrimp creates a jet of water that can travel **62 miles** (100 km/h) an hour.

Algae sometimes grow on sloth fur.

Roman gladiators *consumed an* ***energy drink*** *containing ash.*

SOME 20 BILLION PLANETS IN OUR GALAXY COULD SUPPORT ALIEN LIFE.

AN OREGON **MAN** MADE A **40-FOOT-TALL** (12-m) **NUTCRACKER** THAT CAN **CRACK COCONUTS.**

SCIENTISTS CREATED A **FORK** THAT MEASURES HOW LONG YOU PAUSE BETWEEN BITES TO SHOW *HOW* ***FAST*** *YOU'RE* ***EATING.***

SOME KINDS OF APPLES ARE PINK ON THE INSIDE.

The first steam **locomotive** made in the United States **lost a race to a horse.**

SOME OLD JETS ARE PLACED

IN AIRPLANE GRAVEYARDS.

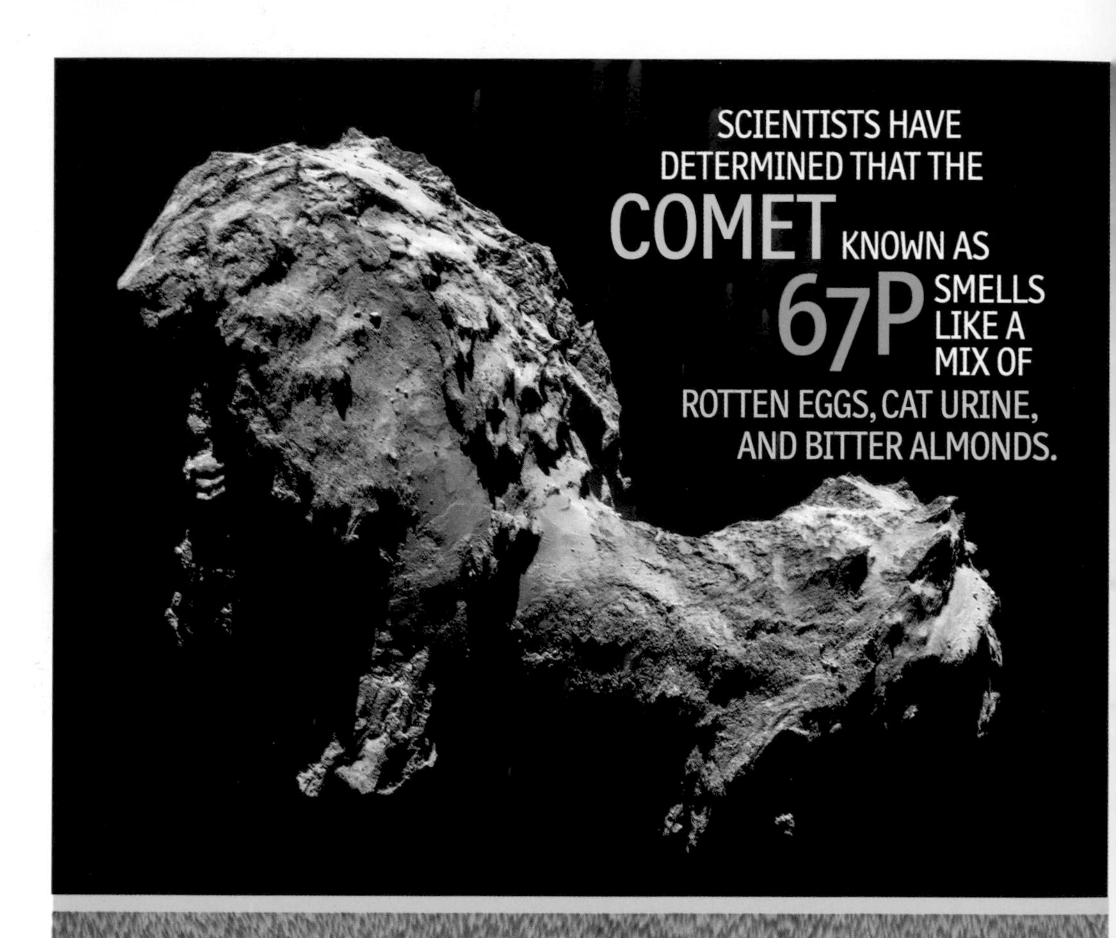

SCIENTISTS HAVE DETERMINED THAT THE COMET KNOWN AS 67P SMELLS LIKE A MIX OF ROTTEN EGGS, CAT URINE, AND BITTER ALMONDS.

CAMELS ARE BORN WITHOUT HUMPS.

HERMIT CRABS COMMUNICATE BY CHIRPING.

Some snakes can see the heat given off by mammals' bodies.

BOXER DOGS SOMETIMES FIGHT BY STANDING ON THEIR HIND LEGS AND BATTING EACH OTHER WITH THEIR FRONT PAWS.

Some worms that live on coral reefs look like tiny, colorful Christmas trees.

Scientists used a robot disguised as a penguin to study real emperor penguins.

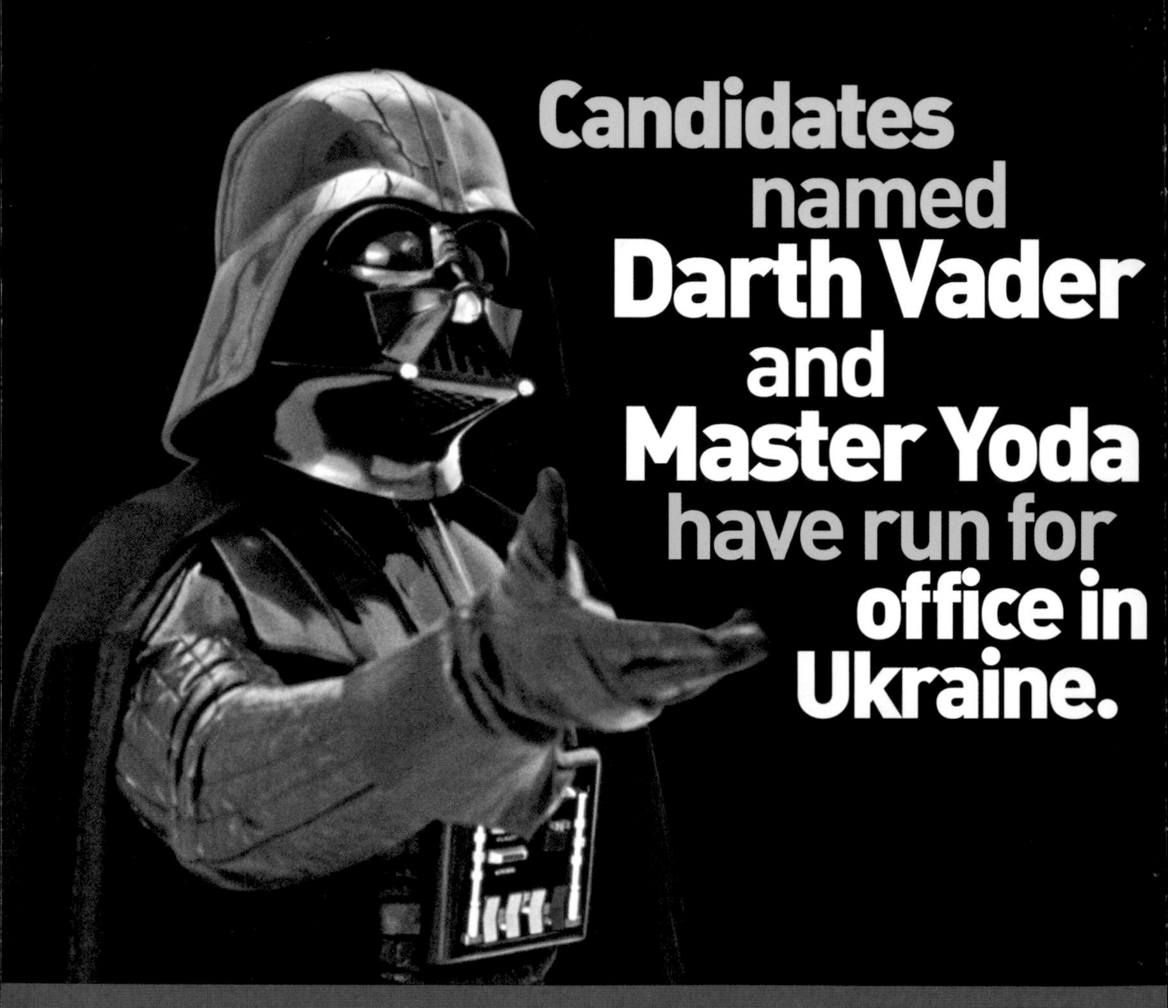

Candidates named Darth Vader and Master Yoda have run for office in Ukraine.

THE LANGUAGE OF THE EWOKS IN *RETURN OF THE JEDI*

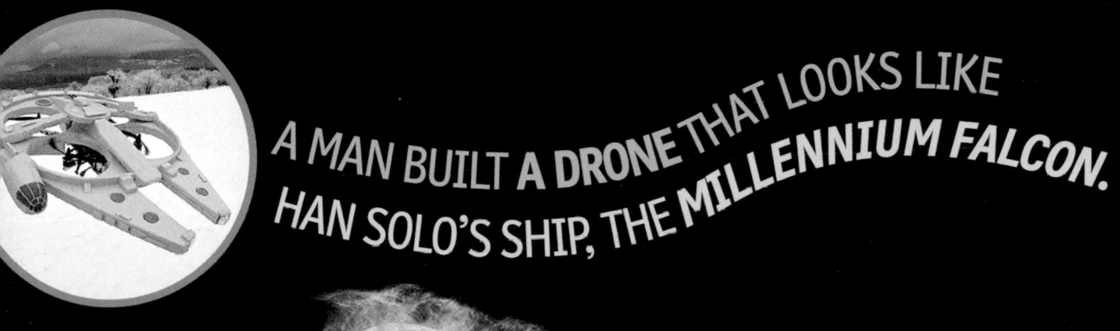

A MAN BUILT **A DRONE** THAT LOOKS LIKE HAN SOLO'S SHIP, THE ***MILLENNIUM FALCON.***

IS PARTLY BASED ON TIBETAN AND NEPALI.

IN 1921,

NEARLY 76 (193 cm) INCHES OF SNOW

FELL IN 24 HOURS ON SILVER LAKE, COLORADO, U.S.A.

One volcano in Indonesia burns with electric-blue flames.

EVERY DAY,
100 TONS OF (91 t)
COSMIC DUST
FROM SPACE
ENTERS EARTH'S ATMOSPHERE—
THAT'S THE SAME WEIGHT AS
400 MOUNTAIN GORILLAS.

HERDS OF
BUFFALO-SIZE
RODENTS
ONCE ROAMED
SOUTH AMERICA.

HONEYPOT WORKER ANTS, WHICH STORE NECTAR IN THEIR BODIES, CAN SWELL TO THE SIZE OF A GRAPE.

Shoppers are more likely to buy a product if they **touch it,** one study found.

THE TEETH OF AT LEAST TWO SHARK SPECIES ARE NATURALLY COATED IN FLUORIDE, A MAIN INGREDIENT IN TOOTHPASTE.

IN SAGADA,
PHILIPPINES,
COFFINS
ARE NAILED TO
A CLIFF FACE
RATHER THAN BURIED
UNDERGROUND.

CUCUMBERS WERE
KNOWN AS
"COWCUMBERS"
UNTIL THE
MID-19TH CENTURY.

LOUISIANA, U.S.A.,
IS HOME TO SOME
500,000
WILD PIGS.

A New York City artist invented a waffle iron that makes waffles shaped like a computer keyboard.

AS A HEN GETS OLDER, SHE PRODUCES BIGGER EGGS.

THE INTERNATIONAL SPACE STATION WEIGHS MORE THAN 300 CARS.

A WARM GOLF BALL WILL TRAVEL FARTHER THROUGH THE AIR THAN A COLD ONE.

Every year, **300 million golf balls** are lost or thrown away in the United States.

GOLF WAS BANNED IN 15TH-CENTURY SCOTLAND.

ONE KIND OF MITE CAN SPRINT 20 TIMES FASTER THAN A CHEETAH, AS MEASURED IN BODY LENGTHS TRAVELED EACH SECOND.

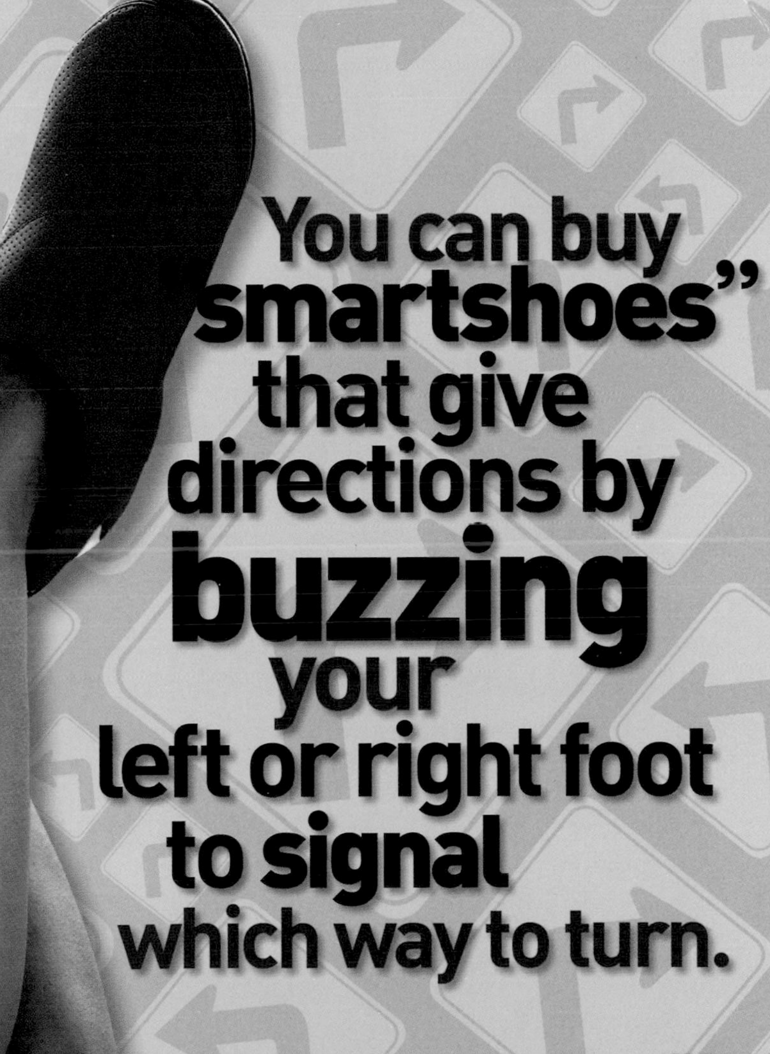

You can buy "**smartshoes**" that give directions by **buzzing** your left or right foot to **signal** which way to turn.

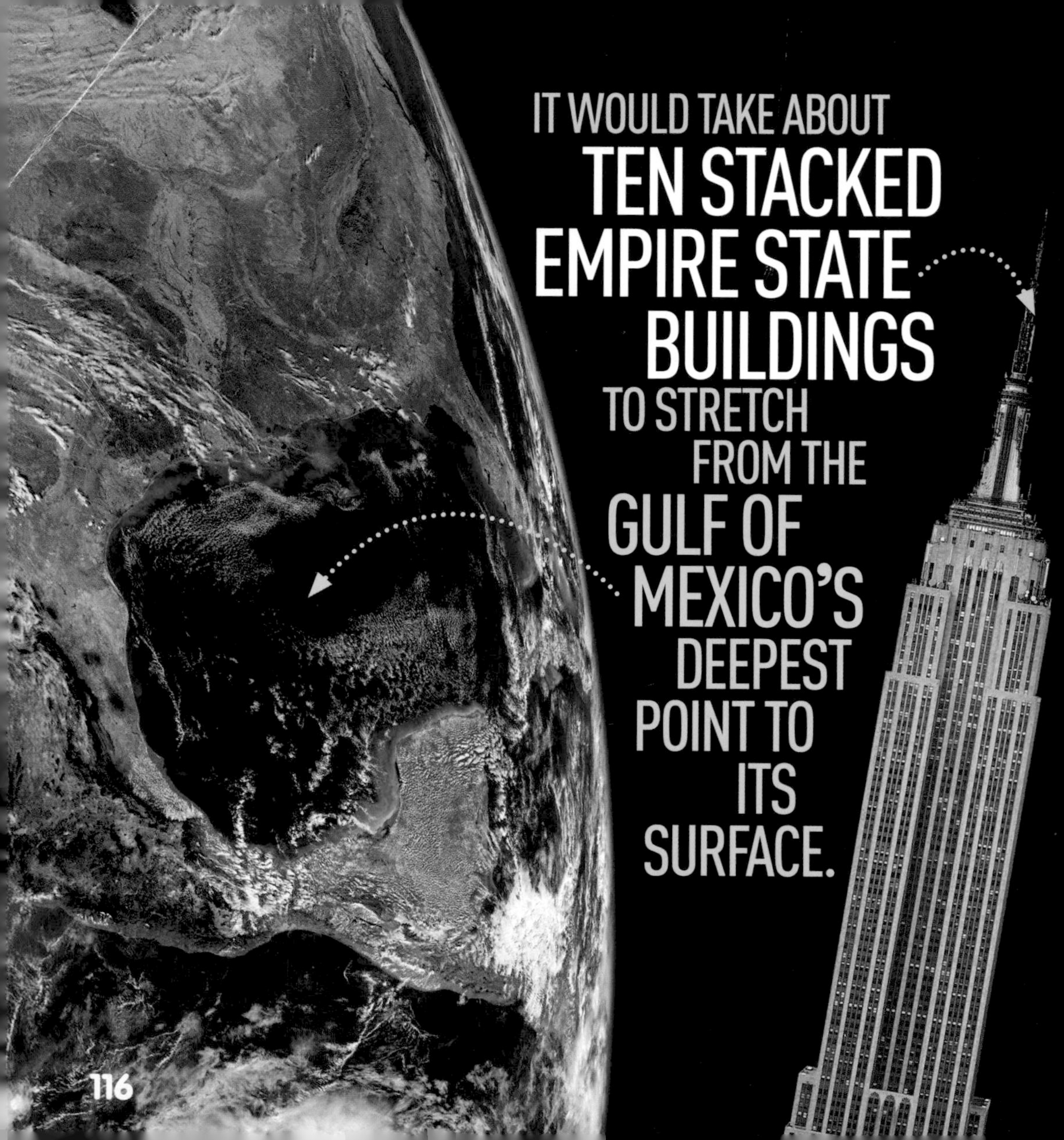
IT WOULD TAKE ABOUT
TEN STACKED
EMPIRE STATE
BUILDINGS
TO STRETCH
FROM THE
GULF OF
MEXICO'S
DEEPEST
POINT TO
ITS
SURFACE.

Crocodiles sometimes climb trees.

WOOF!

ONE TYPE OF OWL IN AUSTRALIA BARKS LIKE A DOG.

ICE SCULPTORS IN TEXAS, U.S.A., RE-CREATED SCENES FROM *FROSTY THE SNOWMAN* USING 2 MILLION POUNDS (907,185 kg) OF ICE.

Grasshopper Glacier in Montana, U.S.A., contains layers of grasshoppers preserved in ice.

Certain radio signals coming from Jupiter sound like popcorn popping.

CURIOUS GEORGE WAS ORIGINALLY NAMED **FIFI.**

SCIENTISTS LANDED A REMOTE-CONTROLLED SPACECRAFT ON A COMET THAT WAS TRAVELING 84,000 MILES (135,185 km/h) AN HOUR.

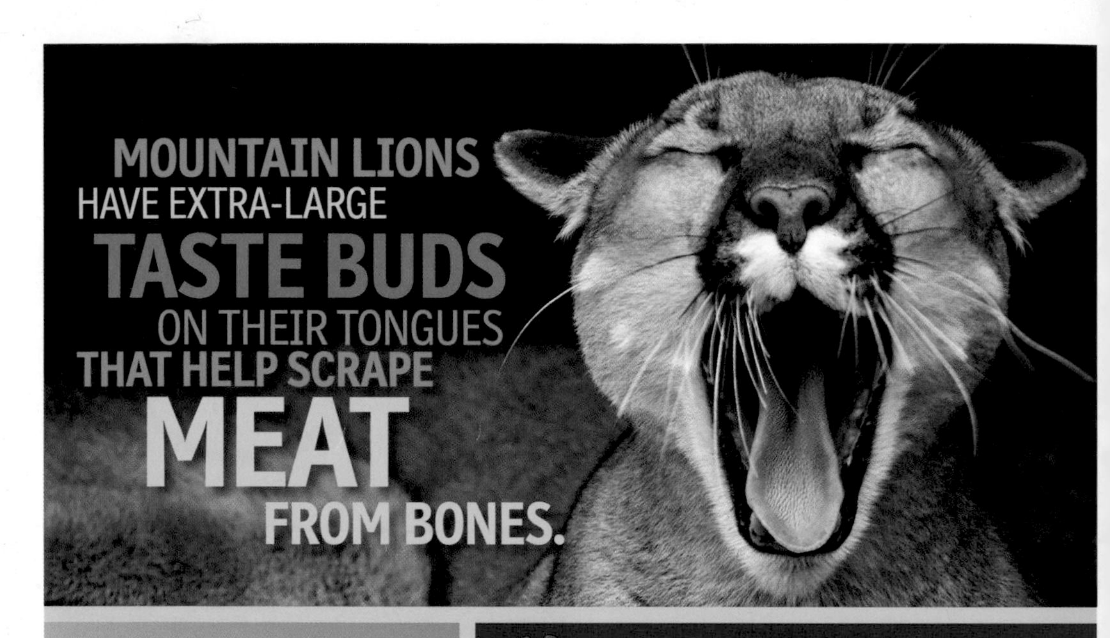

The cruise ship Queen Mary 2 *has a plant that makes freshwater from saltwater.*

The average car has some 25,000 parts.

THE CREATOR OF WONDER WOMAN

ALSO INVENTED AN EARLY VERSION OF THE LIE DETECTOR.

IT TOOK THE INVENTOR OF THE RUBIK'S CUBE MORE THAN A MONTH TO SOLVE THE PUZZLE AFTER SCRAMBLING IT FOR THE FIRST TIME.

THE WORLD'S LARGEST RUBIK'S CUBE IS 17-BY-17-BY-17 CUBES.

Some streets in
Seattle, Washington, U.S.A.,
boast
artwork
that only becomes
visible
when splashed
with
water.

The DISCO CLAM
uses flashes of light reflected
from its lips to ward off predators.

IF BUNDLED TOGETHER, ALL THE BRANCHES OF A TREE WOULD BE ABOUT AS THICK AS ITS TRUNK.

No cars
are allowed on
Sark Island
in the
English
Channel.

THE AVERAGE PENCIL HAS ENOUGH GRAPHITE

AFRICA'S NILE RIVER IS LONGER THAN THE

TO DRAW A LINE THAT'S 35 MILES LONG.

(56 km)

The Tinkerbell wasp is only two and a half times the width of a human hair.

WIDTH OF THE CONTIGUOUS UNITED STATES.

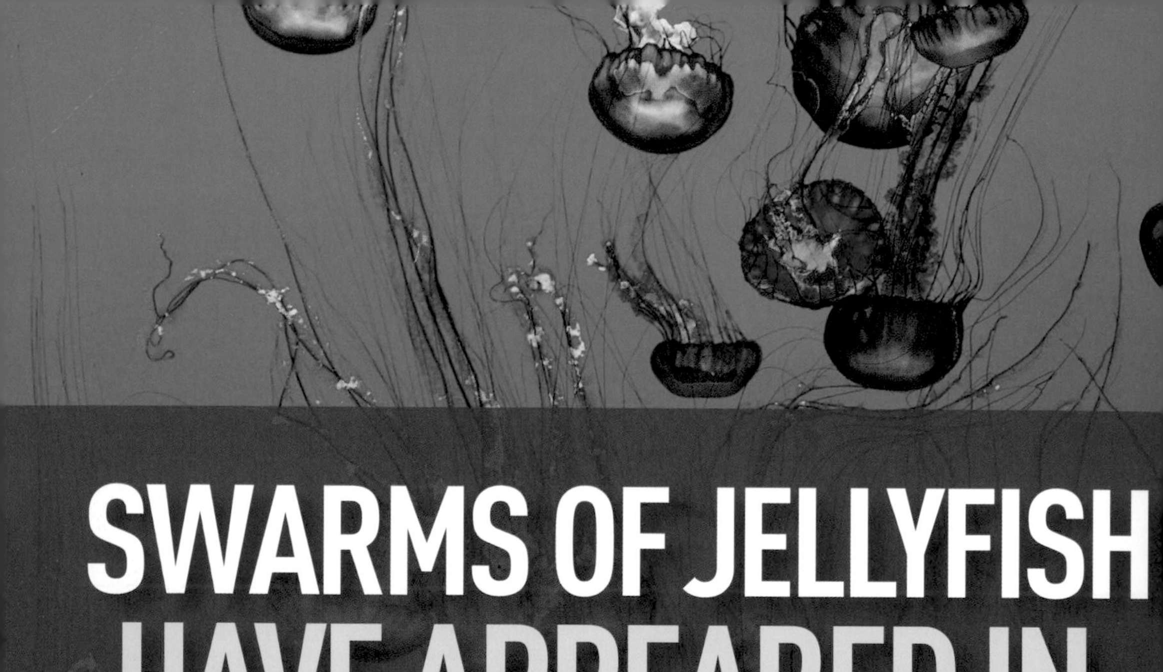

SWARMS OF JELLYFISH HAVE APPEARED IN

(161 km)
STRETCHING 100 MILES
THE GULF OF MEXICO.

THE DIVING BELL SPIDER IS THE ONLY SPIDER THAT LIVES ITS **LIFE** ENTIRELY UNDERWATER.

THE PLANET KEPLER-413B WOBBLES LIKE A *SPINNING TOP.*

A study found that saying "**OW**" can help you tolerate pain better.

SEVERAL **CAVES** IN KENTUCKY, U.S.A., ARE HOME TO A SPECIES OF SEE-THROUGH, **EYELESS SHRIMP.**

NASA'S HUBBLE TELESCOPE CAPTURED AN IMAGE OF A GALAXY CLUSTER THAT LOOKS LIKE A SMILEY FACE.

THE POLICE SQUAD OF ONE SOUTHERN RUSSIAN TOWN IS MADE UP ENTIRELY OF IDENTICAL TWINS AND TRIPLETS.

MORE THAN 100 MILES (161 km) OF MINING TUNNELS EXIST UNDER DETROIT, MICHIGAN, U.S.A.

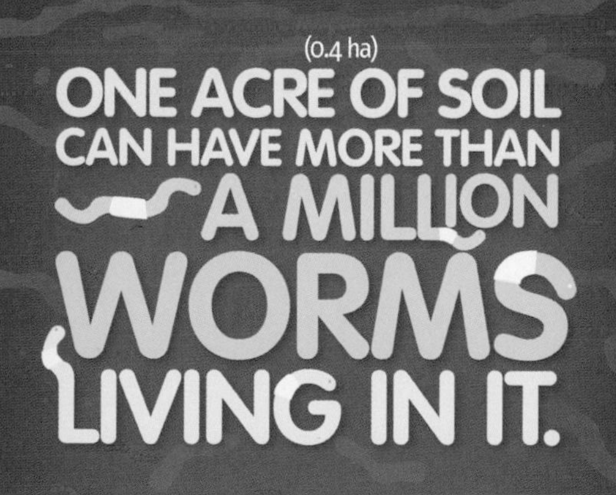

Google used a camel *with a* camera mounted on its hump to help map a desert *in the United Arab Emirates.*

SPRAY FROM AFRICA'S VICTORIA FALLS CAN SHOOT 1,600 FEET IN THE AIR.
(500 m)

To distribute berries, cedar waxwing birds line up and pass them from beak to beak.

MALE EMEI MUSTACHE TOADS GROW A LINE OF SPIKES ALONG THEIR UPPER LIPS.

ANCIENT HAWAIIANS SOMETIMES MADE LEIS OUT OF BONES.

EMPEROR PENGUINS CAN'T TASTE THE FISH THEY EAT.

Inventors used a 3-D printer to produce a working electric car.

MARINE SNAILS' TEETH ARE THE STRONGEST MATERIAL FOUND IN NATURE.

Caribou release an odor from their ankles when threatened.

A more than 500-year-old bed that may have belonged to King Henry VII was recently found in a parking lot in England.

About one-quarter of the world's hazelnut supply is used to make Nutella.

In the United States, more than 20 million tons (18 million t) of salt are spread on snowy roads, parking lots, sidewalks, and driveways each year.

Scientists think that **sperm whales** can detect a **swimmer** more than **one mile** (1.6 km) above them.

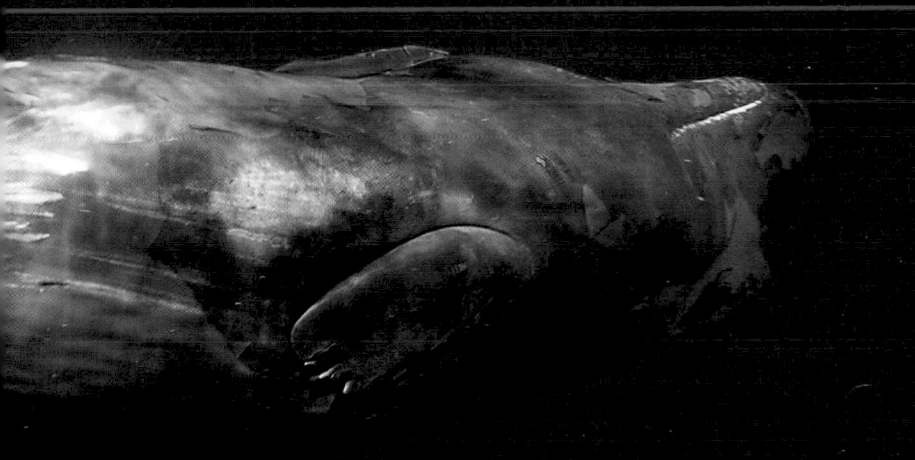

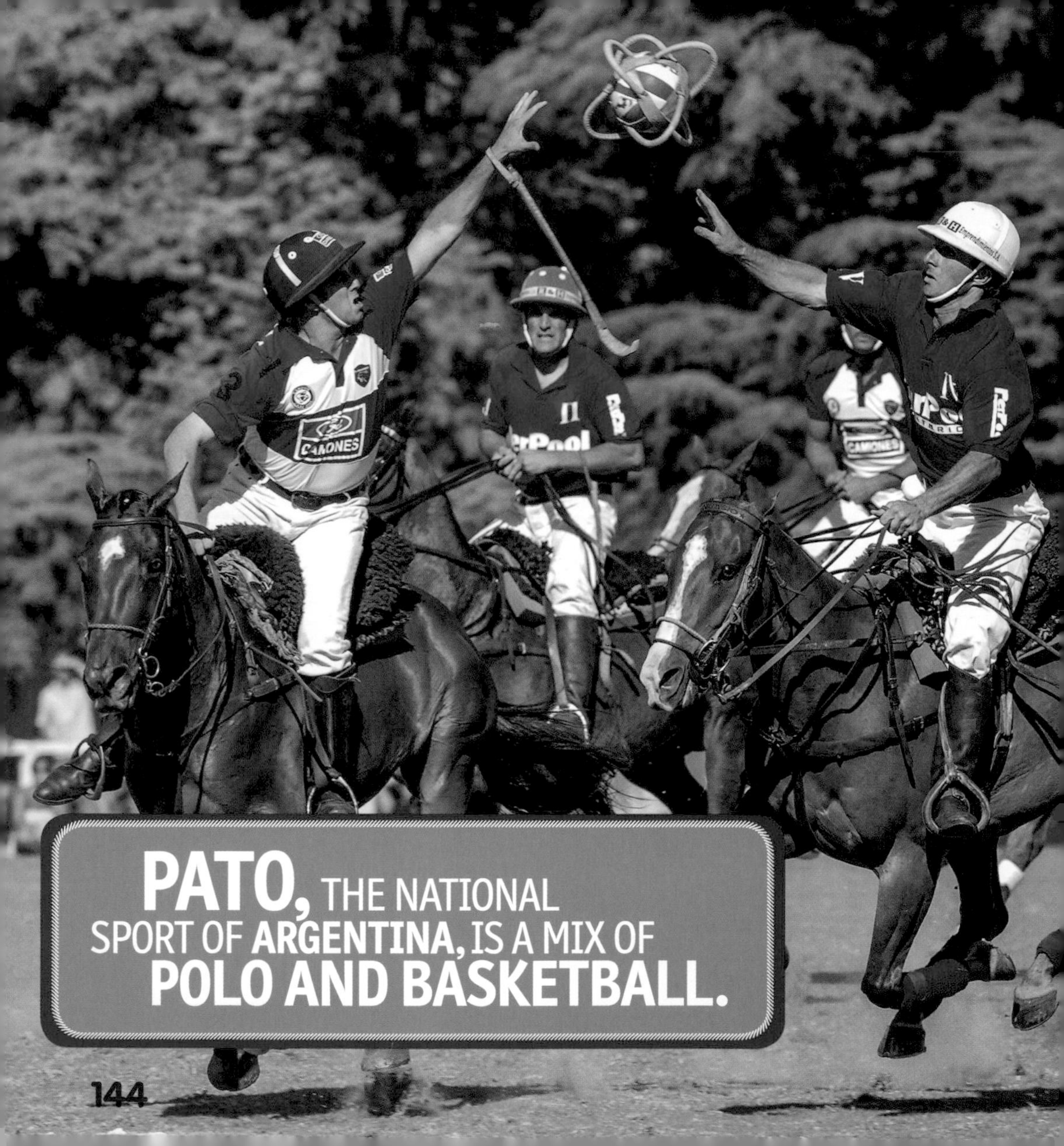

PATO, THE NATIONAL SPORT OF **ARGENTINA,** IS A MIX OF **POLO AND BASKETBALL.**

The average person can recognize about a trillion smells.

The *Titanic* was held together by 3 million rivets.

WATCHING FISH SWIM IN AN AQUARIUM CAN REDUCE STRESS, A STUDY FOUND.

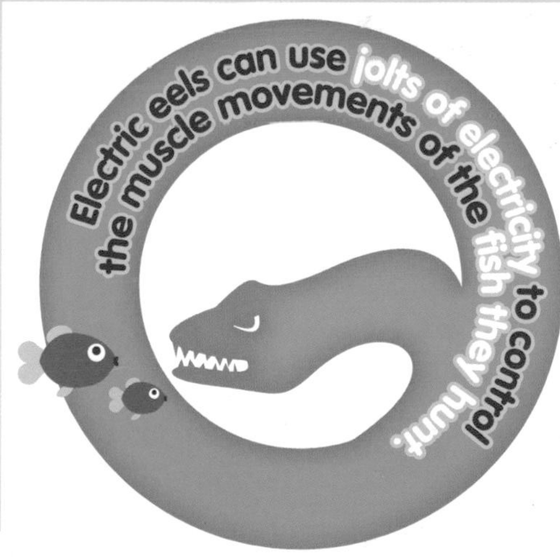

YORKSHIRE
TERRIER
POODLE

YORKIPOO

THE ISLAND OF MAURITIUS IN THE INDIAN OCEAN HAS MULTICOLORED SAND DUNES.

IN 1808, TWO FRENCHMEN FOUGHT A DUEL WHILE FLOATING IN BALLOONS SOME 2,700 FEET (820 m) ABOVE GROUND.

It can take about 25 gallons (95 L) of water to grow one avocado.

The noises Tasmanian devils make when eating can be heard a mile away. (1.6 km)

U.S. FAMILIES SPEND MORE THAN $8 BILLION ON BACK-TO-SCHOOL CLOTHES.

THAT'S FIN-TASTIC!

A GROUP OF SHARKS

IS CALLED A SHIVER.

YOU CAN SEE
TRACTOR
SQUARE DANCES—
WHERE FARMERS MANEUVER TRACTORS
TO MIMIC SQUARE DANCING ROUTINES—
IN THE MIDWESTERN UNITED STATES.

PEOPLE
WHO ARE FREQUENTLY
HUGGED
EXPERIENCE
LESS SEVERE
COLD
SYMPTOMS,
A STUDY FOUND.

Someone who plays
marbles
is called a
mibster.

A HAMSTER'S CHEEK POUCHES EXTEND ALL THE WAY TO ITS hips.

SOME BOWHEAD WHALES LIVE FOR MORE THAN 200 YEARS.

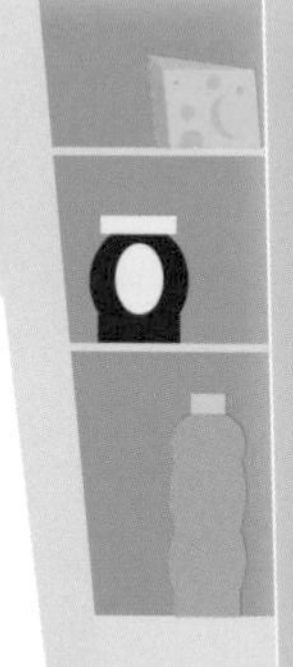

APPLES CAN RIPEN TEN TIMES FASTER AT ROOM TEMPERATURE THAN IN THE REFRIGERATOR.

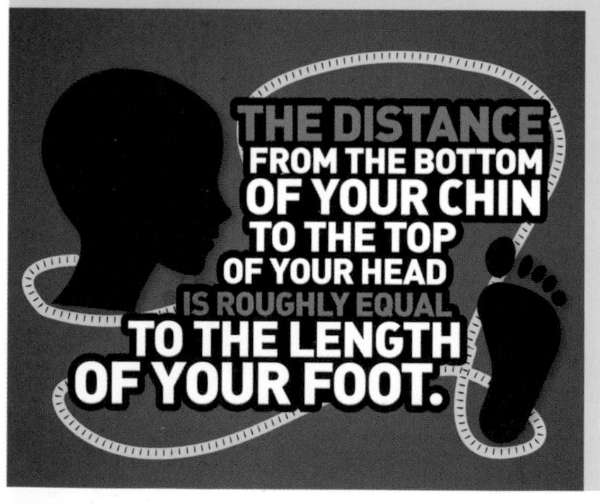

One rock in
Joshua Tree National Park
in California, U.S.A., resembles a
giant human
skull.

A MALE RED DEER'S ANTLERS CAN GROW

TO A WEIGHT OF 60 POUNDS (27 kg) IN THREE MONTHS.

Six of the seven dwarfs in the 1937 animated movie ***Snow White and the Seven Dwarfs*** have eyebrows modeled after Walt Disney's.

Temperatures on Mercury can drop more than 1000°F (550°C) in one day.

A PENNY ISSUED BY THE U.S. MINT IN 1793 SOLD AT AUCTION FOR $2.3 MILLION.
LIBERTY
1793

The first baseball caps were made from straw.

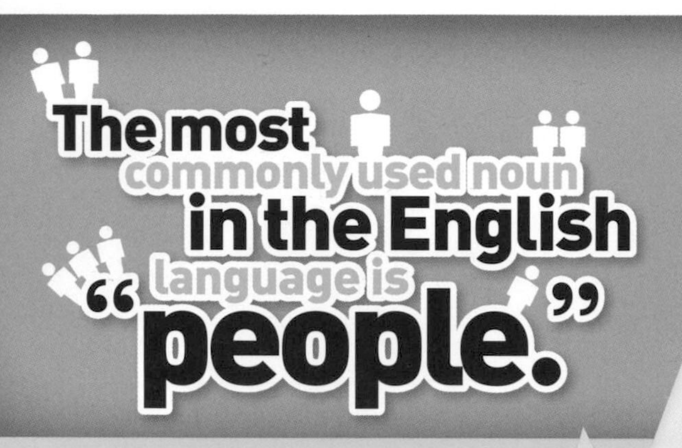

Extreme athletes have skied from the summit of Mount Everest to a base camp 12,000 feet below.
(3,660 m)

Laid end to end, New York City's subway tracks would stretch from the **Big Apple** to Chicago, Illinois, U.S.A.

YOU CAN FIND OVER

2,000 ROCK ARCHES

IN ARCHES NATIONAL PARK,

IN UTAH, U.S.A.

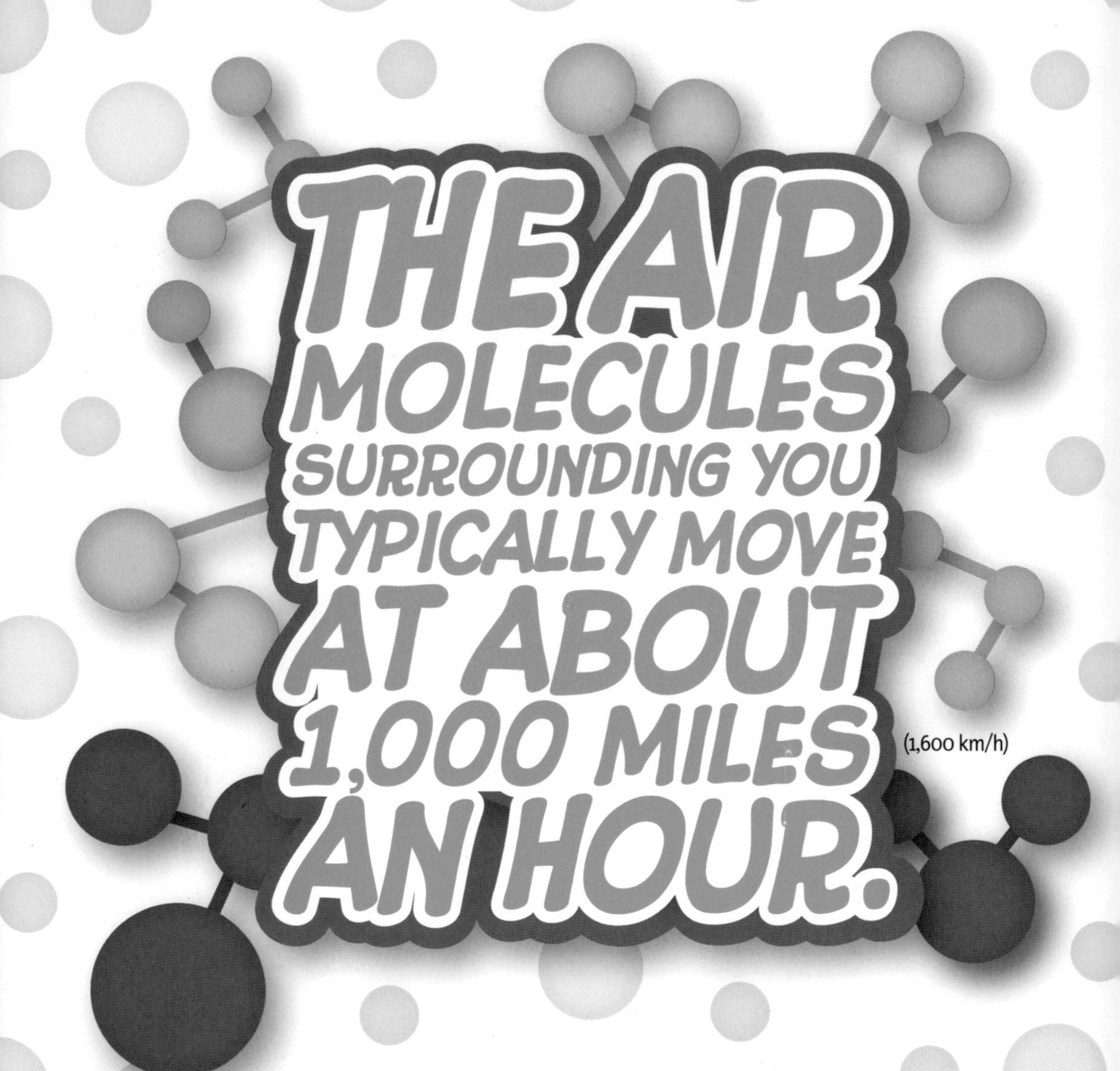
THE AIR
MOLECULES
SURROUNDING YOU
TYPICALLY MOVE
AT ABOUT
1,000 MILES
(1,600 km/h)
AN HOUR.

BOTTLENOSE DOLPHINS SWALLOW THEIR FOOD WHOLE.

IN JAPAN, KFC GAVE AWAY iPHONE CASES SHAPED LIKE GIANT CHICKEN DRUMSTICKS.

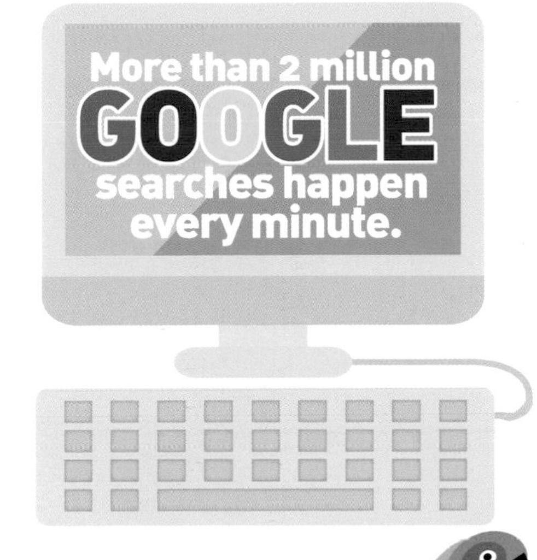

More than 2 million **GOOGLE** searches happen every minute.

The belly button–like formation on a **navel orange** is where another orange is starting to grow.

PARROTS DON'T HAVE VOCAL CORDS!

A newborn sea otter's extra-thick fur traps in so much air that it's impossible for the animal to sink.

SOME SOCCER BALLS HAVE A BUILT-IN CHIP THAT SIGNALS REFEREES WHEN THE BALL PASSES THE GOAL LINE.

3,240 SOCCER BALLS WERE USED DURING THE 2014 WORLD CUP.

PROFESSIONAL SOCCER PLAYERS RUN AN AVERAGE OF SEVEN MILES (11 km) DURING EACH GAME.

AN INDOOR SOCCER MATCH IN ALBERTA, CANADA, LASTED 30 HOURS AND 10 MINUTES.

AN ATLANTIC PUFFIN CAN HOLD AS MANY AS A DOZEN SMALL FISH IN ITS BILL AT ONE TIME.
SOME MOTHS DON'T HAVE MOUTHS.

A BILLBOARD IN RIYADH, SAUDI ARABIA, STRETCHES

THE LENGTH OF NEARLY NINE BASKETBALL COURTS.

AN ARTiST IN LONDON, ENGLAND, CONSTRUCTED A BUiLDiNG THAT APPEARS TO LEViTATE.

A HEDGEHOG HAS ABOUT

Polar bears sometimes communicate by touching noses.

SOME PEOPLE LACK THE GENE THAT CAUSES SMELLY UNDERARMS.

ONIONS AND GARLIC CAN BE USED TO HELP SOAK UP TOXIC SPILLS.

TRISKAIDEKAPHOBIA IS THE FEAR OF THE NUMBER 13.

THE WORLD'S LARGEST DISCO BALL

IS MORE THAN **33 FEET** (10 m) IN DIAMETER— ALMOST AS WIDE AS A TENNIS COURT.

The common
octopus
is the
size of a
flea at birth.

INK FROM THE COMMON **OCTOPUS** CONTAINS A SUBSTANCE THAT DULLS A PREDATOR'S SENSE OF **SMELL.**

SOME **OCTOPUSES** BUILD FORTRESSES OUT OF **SHELLS AND ROCKS.**

SOME 21,000 YEARS AGO, MASSIVE ICEBERGS FLOATED OFF THE COAST OF FLORIDA, U.S.A.

India sent a spacecraft known as MOM to Mars.

Researchers are trying
to develop a car tire
made from dandelions.

More than 1,400 varieties of cheese exist in the world.

CERTAIN **FERNS** EJECT THEIR SPORES WITH A CATAPULT MOTION.

A GROUP OF GIRAFFES

WONDER HOW WE GOT THAT NAME?
IS CALLED A TOWER.

A West Indian manatee's lungs are two-thirds the length of its body.

Your glabella is the area
of skin between your eyebrows.

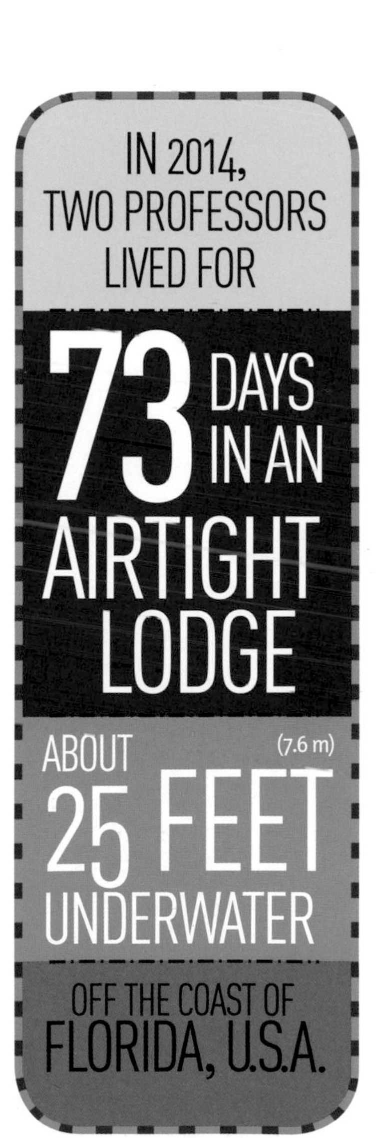

All of Earth's land could fit in the Pacific Ocean.

A SPECIAL TYPE OF

DUMP TRUCK

MADE IN SIBERIA, RUSSIA,

CAN HOLD **550 TONS OF DIRT—** (499 t)

THAT'S AS HEAVY AS A FULLY LOADED 747-8 FREIGHTER PLANE.

The American goldfinch sometimes sounds as if it's saying "po-tay-toe-chip" when it chirps.

WAVES OFF THE COAST OF PUERTO MALABRIGO, PERU, CAN STRETCH MORE THAN A MILE LONG. (1.6 km)

A SINGLE BANANA IS CALLED A FINGER; A BUNCH IS CALLED A HAND.

MALE KANGAROOS FLEX THEIR BICEPS TO IMPRESS FEMALES.

ENOUGH CANDY CORN IS MADE EVERY YEAR TO GIVE EVERY PERSON ON EARTH ONE KERNEL.

89 PERCENT OF PEOPLE EAT A CHOCOLATE

COULD YOU SPEAK UP?
OVER A BILLION CANDY CANES ARE MADE EACH YEAR.
EASTER BUNNY'S EARS FIRST.

FACTFINDER

Boldface indicates illustrations.

D

E

F

G

H

I

J

K

L

Staff for This Book
Andrea Silen, *Project Editor*
Julide Dengel, *Art Director*
Hillary Leo, *Photo Editor*
Paige Towler, *Editorial Assistant*
Sanjida Rashid and Rachel Kenny, *Design Production Assistants*
Michael Cassady and Mari Robinson, *Rights Clearance Specialists*
Grace Hill, *Managing Editor*
Joan Gossett, *Senior Production Editor*
Lewis R. Bassford, *Production Manager*
Nicole Elliott, *Manager, Production Services*
Susan Borke, *Legal and Business Affairs*
John Chow, *Imaging*

Published by the National Geographic Society
Gary E. Knell, *President and CEO*
John M. Fahey, *Chairman of the Board*
Melina Gerosa Bellows, *Chief Education Officer*
Declan Moore, *Chief Media Officer*
Hector Sierra, *Senior Vice President and General Manager, Book Division*

Senior Management Team, Kids Publishing and Media
Nancy Laties Feresten, *Senior Vice President;* Erica Green, *Vice President, Editorial Director, Kids Books*; Julie Vosburgh Agnone, *Vice President, Operations;* Jennifer Emmett, *Vice President, Content;* Michelle Sullivan, *Vice President, Video and Digital Initiatives;* Eva Absher-Schantz, *Vice President, Visual Identity;* Rachel Buchholz, *Editor and Vice President,* NG Kids *magazine*; Jay Sumner, *Photo Director;* Hannah August, *Marketing Director;* R. Gary Colbert, *Production Director*

Digital
Laura Goertzel, *Manager*; Sara Zeglin, *Senior Producer;* Bianca Bowman, *Assistant Producer;* Natalie Jones, *Senior Product Manager*

The National Geographic Society is one of the world's largest nonprofit scientific and educational organizations. Founded in 1888 to "increase and diffuse geographic knowledge," the Society's mission is to inspire people to care about the planet. It reaches more than 400 million people worldwide each month through its official journal, *National Geographic*, and other magazines; National Geographic Channel; television documentaries; music; radio; films; books; DVDs; maps; exhibitions; live events; school publishing programs; interactive media; and merchandise. National Geographic has funded more than 10,000 scientific research, conservation, and exploration projects and supports an education program promoting geographic literacy.

For more information, please visit nationalgeographic.com, call 1-800-NGS LINE (647-5463), or write to the following address:
National Geographic Society
1145 17th Street N.W.
Washington, DC 20036-4688 U.S.A.

Visit us online at nationalgeographic.com/books

For librarians and teachers: ngchildrensbooks.org

More for kids from National Geographic: kids.nationalgeographic.com

For information about special discounts for bulk purchases, please contact National Geographic Books Special Sales: ngspecsales@ngs.org

For rights or permissions inquiries, please contact National Geographic Books Subsidiary Rights: ngbookrights@ngs.org

Paperback ISBN: 978-1-4263-2086-6
Reinforced library binding ISBN: 978-1-4263-2087-3

Printed in China
15/PPS/1

PHOTO CREDITS

ALL ARTWORK BY MODUZA DESIGN UNLESS OTHERWISE NOTED BELOW:

Cover: (hedgehog), American Images/SuperStock; 2, American Images Inc/SuperStock; 4-5, William Anderson/Getty Images; 6 (UP), courtesy Gugliermetto Experience; 6 (LO), STILLFX/Shutterstock; 9, Misja Smits, Buiten-beeld/Minden Pictures; 10-11, SeaPics.com; 12, TIG Media/Peter Glazebrook/Caters News Agency; 15, cnicbc/iStockphoto; 16–17, Mark Newman/FLPA/Minden Pictures; 19, Maya Kovacheva Photography/Dreamstime; 21, Yuccsan Industries JSC/Rex/REX USA; 22, Antgain/iStockphoto; 23, deamles for sale/Shutterstock; 25, courtesy Weta Workshop; 27, Cristian Baitg/Getty Images; 28–29, Architect: Koen Olthuis—Waterstudio.NL, Developer: Dutch Docklands; 30, Piotr Naskrecki/Minden Pictures; 31 (LE), Heinrich van den Berg/Getty Images; 31 (UP AND LO RT), Henrik Larsson/Shutterstock; 32, Hanwha Eagles/YouTube; 33, George McCarthy/Nature Picture Library; 34–35, Raimund Linke/Getty Images; 34, Christi Tolbert/Shutterstock; 37, Evgeniya Uvarova/Shutterstock; 40, AP Photo/David Goldman; 43 (UP), subjug/iStockphoto; 43 (LO), NASA/Asif A. Siddiqi; 45, Eric Isselee/Shutterstock; 46, Cyril Ruoso/Minden Pictures; 47, Kevin Schafer/Minden Pictures; 49, Kevin Schafer/Minden Pictures; 50, James Hager/Robert Harding World Imagery/Corbis; 51, NASA/JPL-Caltech/SSI/Hampton University; 52, Illustration courtesy Gabriel Perez Diaz, Instituto de Astrofisica de Canarias; 56, Tui De Roy/Minden Pictures; 58, Rick Strange/Alamy; 59, Rosa Betancourt/0 people images/Alamy; 60, Stephen Belcher/Minden Pictures; 61, MWA/ZOJ/Michael Wright/WENN.com/Newscom; 62, Miketanct/iStockphoto; 63 (ALL), courtesy Oznoon by Junior Fritz Jacquet/CFSE AGAPE ART; 64–65, Margot Kessler/iStockphoto; 66, David Livingston/Getty Images; 70–71, Joe Alvarez; 72, Europics/Newscom; 73, Elenazarubina/Dreamstime; 74, Al Shibla/Caters News Agency; 75, AridOcean/Shutterstock; 76–77, Paul Nicklen/National Geographic Creative; 78 (LE), Chris Newbert/Minden Pictures; 78 (RT), photo courtesy of Rick Sullivan; 81 (LE), Aprescindere/Dreamstime; 81, maman/Shutterstock; 82-83, ltos/iStockphoto; 84, The Asahi Shimbun/Getty Images; 87, Edwin Verin/Dreamstime; 88–89, Illustrator, Jennifer Hall/courtesy Carnegie Museum, 92, courtesy HapiFork; 93, Iman Khalili; 94–95, Melanie Stetson Freeman/The Christian Science Monitor/Getty Images; 96, NASA; 98, Chris Newbert/Minden Pictures; 99, Newscom; 100, Lucasfilm/Sunset Boulevard/Corbis; 100 (UP), courtesy of Olivier C.; 101 (CTR), Susana Vera/Reuters/Corbis; 101 (RT), Lucasfilm Ltd./Courtesy Everett Collection; 102, Olivier Grunewald; 104, Reg Morrison/Auscape/Minden Pictures; 106–107, Christian Kober/Robert Harding World Imagery; 109, Imagebroker RF/Getty Images; 110, Chris Dimino, Designer; 112, shirophoto/iStockphoto; 113 (BACK), Andresrimaging/iStockphoto; 113 (LO), Steve Allen/Shutterstock; 115, courtesy Ducere Technologies Pvt. Ltd.; 116 (RT), PEDRE/iStockphoto; 116, NASA; 117, Gallo Images/Alamy; 118, Martin Willis/Minden Pictures; 120, Glenn Christopher/Demotix/Corbis; 122, Dean Pennala/Shutterstock; 124, guroldinneden/iStockphoto; 125, courtesy Oskar Van Deventer; 126, Peregrine Church/Rainworks; 130–131, Jorg Hackemann/Shutterstock; 132, Stephen Dalton/Nature Picture Library; 135, Daan Roosegaarde; 137, courtesy Google Maps; 138, ChinaFotoPress/Getty Images; 139, Courtesy Local Motors/Nyko de Peyer; 140 (FRONT), courtesy The Langley Collection; 140 (BACK), Sakarin Sawasdinaka/Shutterstock; 141, Viktorfischer/Dreamstime; 142, Jens Kuhfs/Getty Images; 144, Eduardo Mariano Rivero/Alamy; 147, Arx Pax; 148 (LE), GlobalP/iStockphoto; 148 (RT), vitcom/iStockphoto; 149, Chrystal Moore/Alamy; 150, Oleg Znamenskiy/Shutterstock; 153 (UP), Photononstop RM/Getty Images; 153 (LO), Lucky-photographer/Shutterstock; 154–155, bradlifestyle/Shutterstock; 156, EPA/Chris Gardner/Newscom; 157, Juniors Bildarchiv GmbH/Alamy; 159, Lunamarina/Dreamstime; 160, Mark Raycroft/Minden Pictures; 163, AP Photo/Heritage Auctions; 165, courtesy "Red" Hong Yi; 166, Flickr RF/Getty Images; 169, UIG/Getty Images; 170 (LE), courtesy YUM! Brands; 170 (RT), courtesy YUM! Brands; 172–173, Donald M. Jones/Minden Pictures; 175, David Robertson/Alamy; 178–179, Artist, Alex Chinneck/photographer, Jeff Moore, Covent Garden Piazza, London; 180, SuperStock; 180, American Images Inc/SuperStock; 183, Victor Frankowski/REX/Newscom; 184–185, OceanBodhi/iStockphoto; 185 (LO), diosmic/iStockphoto; 187, Stephen Dalton/Minden Pictures; 190–191, Oleg Znamenskiy/Shutterstock; 192, Jeff Mondragon/Alamy; 194, www.siemens.com/press; 196–197, Dave Watts/Alamy; 198–199 (Background), Pierre Leclerc/Dreamstime; 199 (LE), Kitano/Dreamstime; 199 (RT), Richard Cote/Dreamstime